For Mission:
Developing a Scriptural Vision for Cultural Transformation

eicc
publications

Published by EICC Publications, a ministry of the Ezra Institute for
Contemporary Christianity, PO Box 9, Stn. Main, Grimsby, ON L3M 1M0

For volume pricing please contact the Ezra Institute for Contemporary
Christianity: info@ezrainstitute.ca.

For Mission: The Need for Scriptural Cultural Theology
ISBN: 978-1-989169-01-8

For Mission: The Need for Scriptural Cultural Theology

CONTENTS

INTRODUCTION

To call this short booklet *For Mission* is not an attempt at rhetorically stacking the deck; I know of no serious Christian who would describe themselves as *against* mission as such. And yet, the title is an acknowledgment that means matter as much as ends, and moreover, that words matter. Just as genuine Christians are for justice, truth, and faithfulness, we are all *for* mission, but what is that mission? what are we on mission for – what is the goal? I would suggest that the mission of God's people is ultimately the faithful worship of the triune God in every aspect and sphere of life – as individuals and as families, neighbourhoods, cities, nations and cultures. Human beings are made "to glorify God and to enjoy him forever."[1] The mission of God's people is thus intimately tied to the purpose for which we were created and therefore the biblical teaching of the kingdom of God.

The term 'mission' as I am using it does not refer simply to the practice of churches sending missionaries to other parts of the world (one aspect of the mission) but to the calling and purpose of God's people in the earth. This is clearly a broader and more foundational application of the term, one that includes global missionary work, but which focuses on understanding the way that Christians, as God's vice-gerents, live out the gospel in every area of life.[2] This living out is our mission, our act of worship (cf. Rom. 12:1-2); it finds expression in every area of life, and the way we think about that mission says something important about our understanding both of the nature of worship and of God.

The decline of a robust, full, vital and applied Christianity in the West is clearly evidenced in our society's preponderance of ungodly laws, apostate educational practices, secular political outlook and overtly neo-pagan arts and entertainment, to name just a few areas. As I hope to show in these brief pages, Christians have allowed, and sometimes even been instrumental, in furthering this decline. An impoverished understanding of our mission has increasingly led us to either abandon these key areas of life and culture in the name of true *piety*, or to uncritically adopt or synthesize them with our faith in the name of *relevance* or even wisdom. In either case, we have tacitly accepted an unbelieving view of the world as normative, and once that has happened, we are in urgent need of fundamental redirection and reformation.

Following a squandered lead and brutal defeat in the 1960 NFL Championship Game, Green Bay Packers' head coach Vince Lombardi implemented a training regimen focused on first principles. "Gentlemen," he told the three dozen professional athletes gathered around him, "this is a football."[3] If Western Christians would have any hope of impacting our society with the truth, freedom and beauty of the gospel of Jesus Christ, we need to recollect where we are and what we are here for; we are on a cosmos-sized field of conflict, not for a game, but a battle between the kingdom of light and kingdom of darkness. As such we must be prepared, by God's grace, to get to the root of what our mission is, and if necessary, radically reorient our lives and ministries accordingly.

This is not a cause for despondency, but for hope. Because of the power of the gospel and omnipotent working of the Holy Spirit, there is every reason for confidence that God will win our nations back to himself. But again, means matter, and in God's eternal wisdom he has called and commissioned us, his people, as ambassadors of the kingdom, to make disciples of the nations, teaching them to obey all that he has commanded (Matt. 28:18-20). This is our mission, this is true worship, and we have only begun to recover the full extent of its power, scope and glory.

Churchianity or Christianity

The impact of the Christian faith upon the cultural history of the West is inescapably visible all around us. From the church buildings on every Toronto city block, to the spires at the centre of every English village, the geography of town and country is testament to a once-vital faith. Indeed Christianity's formative religious power is not just around us to observe in buildings and monuments, it continues to actually inhabit the *people* of the Western world, even when they are unaware of it, discreetly hidden in their language, customs and common assumptions. From some of the greatest works of art, literature, music, and architecture that the West ever produced, and which can still thrill the heart, to the names of hospitals and schools – in fact embedded in the mottos of some of the most prestigious universities – the cultural vestiges of Christianity are ubiquitous.

And yet it is no longer controversial to assert that the Christian church has, for the most part, ceased to be a truly moving force in the affairs of Western civilization. As the noted Christian philosopher Calvin Seerveld has put it, "a foreign dynamic and the neo-pagan spirit of the Renaissance is shaping the culture of the world at the moment…but because God and the church are dead to the world there has inevitably come an all-encompassing, frustrating loss of order, certainty and security in the world, and that is disturbing even to those who suppress the truth in unrighteousness."[4]

In recent years, with this clear abandonment of a Christian vision for culture happening at a rapid pace all around us, and the insecurity it has produced, some Christians have been waking up to the fact that there is a pressing and vital question to be asked: what is the nature of the relationship of the gospel of Jesus Christ to the society in which we live? To state the question in a slightly different way, what is the relationship of God's Word-revelation to the Christian's life in the world? It is a sign of hope for the church that there are those who have begun to consider carefully again the character of the relationship between the gospel and culture – perhaps with a degree of urgency not seen in many years. It is a prescient issue, because the conclusions Christians reach will determine the *essential character* of the mission of God's people in our day.

I say this *renewed* interest is a sign of hope because, generally speaking, and admitting of notable exceptions, this subject is one that Western evangelicals have *not* pursued with focused seriousness for several generations. As a result of this revived concern a fresh line of thought is opening up, calling forth an essentially new specialization within theology – *cultural theology*.[5] As my colleague Andrew Sandlin ably explains the expanding opportunity:

An emerging specialty in theology is cultural theology. It is defined as the study of what God's full revelation teaches about culture and applying that teaching to pressing cultural issues. Because the issues of our time have become specialized, the study of revelation must include a specialized concern for culture. Of course, culture has been around as long as man has, and therefore cultural theology is not a specialty whose need has only recently evolved. However, dramatic developments of culture in modern times (in, for example, ideology, technology, jurisprudence, medicine, economics, and the arts) press serious Christians for a coherent grasp of godly truth to address and govern them. For instance, what does God's revelation have to say to the political views known as socialism, liberalism, conservatism, or libertarianism? Or ideologies like Marxism, feminism, Islamism, transgenderism, and white privilege? What about new technologies like stem-cell research, genetic manipulation, cloning, transhumanism, and surrogate motherhood? Consider theories of law: originalism, progressivism, sociological law, utilitarian law, and natural law. These developments, contemporary or traditional, and many others require a distinctly Christian evaluation.[6]

This need, for Christians to turn to God's Word-revelation for clear guidance in such complex matters from the world of everyday cultural experience, simply expresses another aspect of the constant necessity for believers to be both *in*formed – that is, inwardly guided from the centre of their being – and *re*formed, or reshaped, by God's Word when our attitudes and thinking in any area of life are found contrary to that Word.

In this case it must be asked how accurately our attitudes and thinking regarding the gospel's relationship to culture reflects the teaching and concerns of God's *Word-revelation*.

THE THREE INTERRELATED SENSES OF THE "WORD OF GOD"

To speak in this way about the Word-revelation of God is to confess that in every area of our lives, we are *subject* to that Word. That confession addresses three primary realities. First, we are subject to the *creation Word* of God which called all things into being and holds all things together. We daily encounter the power and glory of God's Word for creation. Creation is a concretization or instantiation of the powerful Word of God. In it we discern laws and norms that God has established for all creation from the very beginning. The mediator of that creation Word is the eternal Son (John 1:1-5). *Secondly*, Jesus Christ is the *incarnate Word* of God. As the second person of the godhead, he is the historical manifestation of the Word through whom all things were made. And *thirdly*, the Bible holds a central place in the Christian life because it is the *inscripturated Word* of God that tells us of the person of Christ, his creative and redemptive work in history, *republishing* the norms of the creation Word so as to make crystal clear in a fallen world what God requires of us.

All three of these manifestations of the *Word of God* are involved in each other, presuppose one another, and cannot be artificially divided or separated from one another as we address the relationship of God's Word to culture; in fact they cannot be properly understood except as a *unity* within a coherence of meaning established for creation by God. For example, we see in all forms of false teaching that a Christ separated from his creative work and the scriptures produces an imaginary Jesus in the likeness of sinful man's desires. Equally, the Bible abstracted from the concrete world of creation and history or from the living and resurrected Lord is reduced to just another piece of human literature. And in the same way, a cosmic order separated from the eternal Son of God and his inscripturated Word is reduced by philosophers and scientists to a mass of sensory data (or 'brute facts') and formal abstract ideas impervious to true interpretation without unity or coherence of meaning. To properly understand God's *world* we need both the Word *incarnate* and *inscripturated,* otherwise the criterion for true insight into the meaning of all things is lost. The unity of God's Word to us in creational and redemptive revelation speaks volumes about the *undivided character* of our calling in the world in terms of that Word.

THE NEED FOR A SCRIPTURAL THEOLOGY *AND* PHILOSOPHY OF CULTURE

Because the *Word of God* is of this creative, formative and unitive character, it is that which must constitute the foundation of *all* truly Christian thought for each area of life. This is crucial because many of the questions being raised by *cultural* theologians are different from those of the more familiar disciplines like dogmatic or systematic theology. Some might say that these questions belong equally, or perhaps particularly, to the domain of philosophy and are therefore part of the task of developing a Christian *philosophy* of life and culture. I am not concerned to quibble over these classifications except to suggest that the questions dealt with in theology and philosophy cannot be neatly separated from each other into hermetically sealed domains that never touch or overlap. This is because theology will always be carried out in terms of underlying concepts and categories of thought that have a philosophical and religious character. Underlying both disciplines – theology and philosophy – is a fundamental *religious orientation* and faith perspective that for the Christian must be controlled and directed by the Word of God. Moreover, it is a grave mistake to think that it is only the professional theologians who can have genuine access to the truth of the Word and be permitted to apply it to the world.

Philosophy, looking at the *totality* of reality, asks about the true nature, origin and relationship of all things and events – Scripture declares the fundamental *answer* to that question, which answer must govern Christian thought in philosophy. At the same time, Christians need to grapple with all the particular challenges within the culture from a robustly *scriptural* standpoint, and so must examine the biblical material as a *starting point*. And so in a very real way, the task before the church is one of developing a faithful cultural *theology,* because we are dealing with our *faith*, the *teaching of Scripture* and our *confession of Christ* as these relate to the culture around us. Christian theology and philosophy need to work together, in submission to God's inscripturated Word, in this endeavor. So whether we characterize this task as working out a scriptural cultural *theology* or *philosophy* is less important than articulating clearly for the church in our time the relationship of God's Word and gospel to culture itself. Until we do that there will be confusion in the church about the Christian mission and an ongoing decline of the impact of our faith on society.

TWO DOMINANT TENDENCIES REGARDING THE MISSION OF GOD'S PEOPLE

It should come as no surprise that something is amiss amongst modern evangelical churches, whether Reformed, charismatic, Pentecostal, Baptist or any other stripe. They are not providing an adequate or consistent response to the challenges of an increasingly anti-Christian culture. On the whole, evangelical leaders seem poorly prepared to equip God's people for the pressing task of applying biblical truth to all of life in an often hostile cultural context – indeed part of the problem is that not all are agreed whether we *should* apply scriptural truth to all areas of life and thought.

I discern two common tendencies in response to the question of the gospel's relationship to culture, and by extension the mission of God's people who declare and live that gospel in the world, and they are linked by common root problems. These tendencies in the church today can be seen first in those who greatly overrate the place and role of the *institutional church* and its offices – thus neglecting or even rejecting the idea that other spheres, institutions and forms of cultural life are realms subject to God's Word. Second, there are those who greatly overrate the role of the *state* (or political life in general) and its responsibilities and functions in working out the kingdom purposes of God in history.

In the first case the visible *institutional church* is essentially identified and conflated with the city and kingdom of God and so what develops, despite a common insistence that they are 'gospel-centred', is a radically *church-centred* faith – what I am calling *churchianity*. This group is at best disinterested in Christ's *manifest* Lordship over any other sphere of life or institution, and at worse they are hostile to it. Those in this camp are normally biblically orthodox in soteriology (the doctrine of salvation) whilst pietistic and often retreatist when it comes to culture. In general they want little or no engagement with society, arts and civil government from a *distinctly* Christian standpoint – especially in the areas of law and education – and any talk of redeeming or transforming culture is seen as out of bounds.

To the extent that these leaders do engage culturally, their involvement is usually described as being for the purposes of 'evangelism' rather than for any broader kingdom purpose or cultural good in its own right. At the very least such non-ecclesiastical activities are carefully distinguished in such a manner as to disclose that they are not 'gospel issues'. For these believers 'the gospel' essentially refers to a narrow set of affirmations about the cross, the new birth, the justification of individuals and their escape from hell. The immediate result is the truncation of the Christian mission to the task of getting more people saved and *into the church*, so that they can go to heaven. To such believers, the Christian life is reduced to personal evangelism, personal piety, personal growth and personal blessing. The Christian calling to seek first the kingdom of God, his righteousness (Matt. 6:33), and the *reconciliation of all things* to him, is conspicuously diminished in this paradigm. There are obvious elements of truth in this position regarding the importance of justification, the new birth and God's final judgment on sin, and this obviously *includes* the salvation of individuals; but is it really a full-orbed and robustly biblical Christianity?

This pietistic but broadly theologically conservative worldview produces immature believers, attending churches where they can remain unchallenged week after week, calling on God for personal blessing or to increase their faith and obedience, but with little or no conception of the scope and grandeur of the gospel or the transforming power of the kingdom of God for all of life. Christians in this context can remain spiritual infants all their lives. The birth of a baby is a wonderful thing, but it would be a tragedy if a baby did not mature over the years into an adult. Such church communities are often marked by frustration and cultural impotence, where congregants are endlessly urged to 'be holy' whilst waiting for the parousia. Yet the average congregant has little or no idea of how to *relate* his faith in Christ the Lord, the scriptures and the call to holiness (i.e. to sanctify life to God) to his marriage and family, his children's education, his vocation, recreational pursuits or civic responsibility – in short, to culture. Salvation, he is told, is for his soul and inner life, whilst the kingdom of God is something that is really coming at the end of the world and so belongs to another age. As a result, the church institute is progressively viewed as the *only place* where God's rule and Christ's lordship are expressed in the earth, especially in the form of the spiritual disciplines of individual Christians, congregational worship and liturgy. Furthermore, on this view, to really serve God or be 'in ministry' means either being a pastor, holding office in the institutional church, or being involved in some activity governed and prescribed by the church. As such there is a glaring and radical sacred/secular divide running through the whole life of such Christians.

At the other end of the spectrum, in the *second* grouping, we have a growing tendency within professing evangelicalism, especially amongst the young, to greatly *underrate* the importance of the institutional church and its administration of the sacraments, the preaching of God's Word and church discipline. Here respect for church confessions, historic teaching and authority is dangerously minimized or set aside in favour of a free-wheeling antinomian approach where the church's institutional role and government in the Christian life is seen as unnecessary or outmoded – a patriarchal religion of life- and freedom-sapping formalism.

These professing Christians rightly detect a problem with cultural abandonment and retreatism in the churches in which they often grew up, perceiving that the gospel must involve more than the salvation of 'souls,' being present for worship on Sunday, getting the liturgy right and attending the Wednesday night Bible study for personal discipleship. They believe that God's kingdom must be broader than the walls of the church, one's personal prayer life and piety; that it must impact the world for the good in real and tangible ways in the here and now.

At the same time, however, the tendency amongst these believers, in questioning whether a pious and retreatist gospel is big enough, is to shift the locus of hope and focus of life from the *church institute* to the institute of the *state* and its powerful apparatus; its civil laws and equalities legislation – that is, to a political enactment of 'social justice.' Under the guiding influence of humanistic philosophy, social action, or what has been dubbed a 'social gospel,' start to replace the centrality of Christ's atoning death, resurrection and life-giving power.

As a consequence, the kingdom of God is increasingly identified with persons, movements and institutions pursuing social and economic 'equality,' so that a kind of politicization of salvation occurs, with the state functioning as *de-facto* high priest in bringing about a secularized deliverance from oppression. Moralism and social action thus gradually eclipse justification by faith in Christ through God's grace alone, whilst a God-centred inward renewal producing outward transformation is replaced by external political coercion as the route to the kingdom. The church institute, its preaching and sacraments, then become almost peripheral to the so-called 'main task' of saving abstract political identity groups like 'the poor' and ending abstract social evils like 'inequality' for the oppressed and other alleged victims of discrimination or exploitation – including the planet itself.

Creation care, service to people in genuine need, and a heart for those oppressed by injustice are of serious concern in Scripture; however, the underlying philosophy that informs a Christianized drive for 'social justice' is *not* scripturally rooted, resulting in a revised version of the Christian lexicon, where the same words are imbued with very different meanings. Thus these Christians regularly drift in a theologically liberal direction – as witness the Emergent Church movement. In extreme cases the gospel of Christ becomes directly identified with egalitarian progressive political philosophy where God's law and Christ's Lordship in terms of Scripture play little or no part. Instead of a familial and moral commitment to voluntary charity and social responsibility, we see political controls, punitive laws of confiscation, as well as judicial activism toward social and sexual liberation put forward as the answer for realizing 'the kingdom of God.' In fact for some the gospel becomes practically indistinguishable from the neo-Marxist, utopian vision of 'humanization' for the biosphere by politics.

Both of these bifurcating tendencies in modern evangelicalism – one identifying the kingdom with the church institute, the other with the political life and social planning of the state – share common root problems. The *first* is a failure to rightly identify the *foundation* of the Christian hope, which is neither the church institute itself nor the state and its activity, but the salvation and lordship of Jesus Christ *himself* over the *totality of life* as the one mediator between man and God. Both the church and the state are institutions with offices placed under God and his sovereignty which limit their role, power and function. The very concept of an office in human culture presupposes service to a broader purpose and higher authority.

The *second* problem is a mischaracterization of the nature of the church and the state, and thereby of the church's mission. The church institute cannot be directly identified with the kingdom of God and therefore the Christian's calling extends well beyond the ministry of the church institution. To limit the kingdom of God to the church is to surrender culture to the enemies of God. As the Christian thinker S.U. Zuidema put it, 'He who ecclesiasticizes God's covenant makes the kingdom of God, insofar as he is able, sectarian because he restricts it to a section of life.'[7] At the same time, however, the church is an important *part* of the kingdom. It cannot be made peripheral to the kingdom by reducing it to a servant or chaplain of the humanistic state, doing its bidding, where scientific socio-political planning is confused with the kingdom of God. Instead the church must witness scripturally and prophetically to political power. When it becomes a handmaiden of the state and an advocate of liberal progressivism (social justice) rather than biblical righteousness, it has forsaken its true character. Likewise, the state overreaches and violates its delimited role and office when, in parts-to-whole fashion it seeks to absorb other spheres of life as departments of state, subject to state planning, control and manipulation.

A *third* problem, which has been with the church from the time Greek philosophy impacted its theological development in the early centuries, is an implicit and destructive dualism that slices up reality into matter and spirit, nature and grace, secular and sacred, natural and supernatural, time and eternity, higher and lower, with one area perceived as lesser or evil and the other as higher and good. This tendency has resulted in a radical separation of creation and redemption (where redemption is essentially for the higher storey of existence), spiritual life and historical-cultural development and mutually reinforcing pattern of *subservience* to non-Christian culture (nature/secular) on the one hand, and the *abandonment* of Christian culture-building (grace/sacred) on the other. Both tendencies emphasize a part of this artificial duality.

Surely to truly grasp who Christ is, as the root of all truth and meaning, is to grasp the universal lordship of Christ and his marvelous call to his church to participate as co-workers with him in the restoration of all things to God – since we are now in Christ and have been given a ministry of reconciliation (2 Cor. 5:19-20). As Seerveld has put it:

> The totality of creation's meaning lies singly in Jesus Christ and his body. And this idea, that the meaning of the individual and universe, lies beyond both in the Son of God, that everything is meaning-*less,* aim-less, vain unless it be set in Jesus Christ, that the crown of creation, humanity, because justly commanded by God to love the Lord with all our heart, all that is in us, that humanity is meaning-*full* only if at work in the covenantal community of believers serving the realization of God's plan, re-creation, reconciliation of all to God through Christ: it is this idea...[which shows] that the

struggle of history is between a newborn *civitas Dei* and the age-old dragons, *civitates mundi*.[8]

Given the clear biblical teaching concerning the person of Christ as the one from whom, through whom and to whom all things exist (Rom. 11:36), and knowing that he is reconciling everything to God the Father (Col. 1:16-20), why is it that Christians seem to struggle to reach agreement about the mission of God's people?

The message of the gospel is therefore centred in the declaration that this Jesus Christ is Lord and King over all the earth, over all cultures, peoples and lands (cf. Matt. 28:18-20) and that he is calling all people to repentance and joyful obedience to the coming kingdom of God.

AN EXAMPLE OF CHURCHIANITY

In this volume my primary concern is to address, not the advocates of social justice (which I have considered in detail elsewhere),[9] but the pietistic cultural retreatism amongst those who are largely theologically orthodox and who are advocates of a kind of *churchianity* – which I want to contrast with scriptural *Christianity*.[10] For the sake of clarity it will help us to begin the discussion of *churchianity* with a typical example of how this problem manifests itself when the calling of Christians and the church in the world is discussed. In a recent interview titled 'On the Mission of the Church,' the popular American pastor, Mark Dever, attempts to articulate the essence of the Christian's gospel-centred calling given the challenges in the culture.[11] The program is very instructive as an illustration of what I have called *churchianity.*

In a series of pithy statements, the sincerely evangelical Dever declares that the sum total of the Christian's calling is to 'make disciples' and 'build churches.' "The Church" is not clearly defined in the discussion, nor is the actual nature and scope of disciple-making. Dever is clear, however, that the central calling of the Christian is *evangelism*, by which he means telling people about Jesus so that they can be forgiven, saved from hell, and join the church. No distinction is made between the life and work of the church institute and the kingdom of God. According to Dever, *"Christianity goes forward by pastors raising up other pastors and sending them out."* Well and good for pastors, but where does this vision of Christian mission leave parents and families, school teachers and truck drivers, business leaders and politicians, lawyers and doctors, housewives and farmers, scholars and architects, musicians and artists, cooks and builders, in the biblical calling to advance the gospel, other than attending church services, being a 'witness' and going to Bible study?

Given Dever's implicit identification of the church institute with the kingdom of God, Christians, he argues, are certainly allowed to *pray* about 'life issues' and for 'local schools' etc., but their real work as God's people is evangelism and discipleship. Dever suggests he is all for parents being involved with the lives of their children and supporting marriage, but that does not mean he assumes we can work to impact social problems like gambling or reduce divorce rates in society. In any case, if the pastor attempts that with his time, he asks, who will preach *the gospel*?

When Dever is specifically asked whether he would ever use the language of 'redeeming culture' or 'transforming the city', he answers forcefully, 'No!' that would only discourage people, he argues, since Dever sees no indication in the scriptures that cultural transformation is promised when Christians preach and live out the gospel. This is an incredible assertion for any student of Scripture to make. The following scriptures warrant a serious consideration in regard to the transforming impact of God's Word in our lives and in cultural life: Genesis 1:26-28; Psalm 2; 8; 110:1-4; Isaiah 9:7; Daniel 2:46-49; 3:26-30; 4:34-36; 6:18-28; Jonah 3:5-10; Habakkuk 2:14; Matthew 28:18-20; Luke 13:18-21; John 12:20-32; 2 Corinthians 5:17-21; Ephesians 1:10, 15-23; Colossians 1:15-20; Hebrews 2:6-13; Revelation 1:4-6. These illustrative texts concerning God's sovereignty, the calling of the covenant people and Christ's authority, power and expanding kingdom, clearly lead us to expect (as has been seen in the past) great cultural impact when believers are walking in obedience to God and serving the purposes of Christ's reign which culminates in the consummation of his kingdom (Rom. 8: 22-23; Rev. 21:5).

Following his denial that the Bible teaches cultures will be transformed by the gospel, it is disappointing to hear Dever and Leeman engage in disparaging the venerable Abraham Kuyper and the vision he articulated of the Lordship of Christ transforming all of life. Dever asks what good either these teachings or Kuyper's tenure as Prime Minister ever did the Netherlands. This is an astonishingly short-sighted attitude toward Kuyper's remarkable and influential legacy; Dever appears to believe that because there are lots of Christians being faithful in various places yet not seeing big changes in public cultural life, cultures aren't changed by the gospel. This belief is a non-sequitur and lacks insight into what is happening at the religious *root* of life when a person's heart is reoriented by the Holy Spirit to serve Christ with all their being. Is the open hostility to a faithful Christian politician (and theologian) like Kuyper the result of Dever's restriction of the gospel to a limited section of life? Zuidema is to the point: "an integral Christian politics, an integral Christian view of the state…which as such play up to neither the ecclesiasticization nor the secularization of life outside of the church – these are a thorn in the flesh for the ecclesiasticized church-man and the politicized politician."[12]

The inescapable reality is that human beings are cultural creatures. Everything we do in and with God's creation is a work of culture-making, and therefore the salvation of an individual and their subsequent faithfulness to God in their personal and family life *does* effect an immediate change in culture as they live in the world. The culture of the home is altered when a man surrenders his life to Christ. The culture of a business begins to change when its leader orients his heart towards God's Word. The culture of a school begins to change when the head teacher turns to Christ and is directed by the scriptures. Indeed, everything in which the true believer is involved, as they live out the truth in terms of God's Word, is powerfully impacted. Yet Dever states with satisfaction that he has had political figures come to him at his Washington D.C. church saying they thought they had come to the capital to impact politics as Christians, but they had since realized at Dever's church that they really had been brought to Washington to learn about *being church* and a good disciple. The *church-centred* character of Dever's understanding of the gospel is thus reinforced in the starkest terms.

Dever certainly affirms Christ's Lordship as a theological *idea*, but materially and practically, for everyday life outside of the church, it fades from view. This is because, as far as Dever is concerned, he can just cooperate and collaborate with non-believers in all the 'ordinary stuff' of life, since he sees no directional distinction in what believers and non-believers are doing in their everyday activities. Thus for Dever, there is no need for, nor indeed is there any such thing as, Christian newspapers, trade unions, etc., and there is certainly no need for Christian political parties and institutions. Naturally he also argues it is simply wrong to say the true way to educate children is *Christian* education. The goal of *Christianizing* anything for Dever is badly misguided – though he never actually clearly explains why.

There is a profound irony in American pastors using their pulpits and religious freedom to attack the Christianization of culture and the application of Scripture to the totality of life, given that their nation was effectively founded by evangelical puritans and was radically shaped throughout its history, in all its public institutions, by Christianity – Moses himself being engraved on Supreme Court buildings. In fact, it was the Christianized nature of American culture, however imperfect, that gave men like Dever their freedom to be pastors and to witness to the gospel without legal hindrance. Moreover there is a disturbing presumption and arrogance that attends church leaders identifying the church institute with the kingdom of God. Zuidema's challenge here is profound and searching:

> The sin of identification of church with the kingdom of God, of church with Covenant, of church with heart religion, whereby for all intents and purposes this church as it were coincides with itself and Christ coincides with the church, is all the more serious since it once and for all blocks the Christian's freedom and the free reign of God's Word over the ecclesiastical offices. Humanly speaking, nothing is so stubborn and so hopeless, so tyrannical and so anarchistic, because nothing is so pious seemingly as this ecclesiasticizing of the Bible and religion.[13]

Despite the privilege of a remarkable Christian heritage in the United States, Dever piously argues that the future will surely be dark, like the days of Noah. As such, instead of speaking of cultural transformation he says, "I wish you would just share *the gospel* with that person on the bus." In this statement we see the appearance of a radically truncated gospel and clear question-begging regarding the nature of the gospel mission – which is in fact the matter in question. It is certainly true that the calling of the church is centred in the gospel. But what is the nature and character of the gospel of the kingdom and what are its implications for us as God's people? Do they go beyond personal evangelism and adding people to the institutional church?

Dever's conclusion regarding the mission of the church is that we don't redeem and transform anything cultural. Thus, his objective is to spend time and resources to *establish churches* that will do witnessing and discipleship. Again, these are no doubt critical tasks for Christians. But for Dever *this alone* is what advances Christianity. We have in this interview then a very good example of what I am arguing is modern and popular evangelical *churchianity*. Calvin Seerveld's caution is telling:

> Many Christians have been content to witness to the world, vigorously preaching Christ crucified but holding back from involvement in the culture because it is so immoral and demoralizing…, yet it is not the full gospel. It has the ascetic reticence of John the Baptizer who preached repentance from sin and counseled moral rectitude in whatever profession you were in, but stopped there. John the Baptizer's disciples fasted, and Christ did not condemn it; He just commanded his disciples who freely ate and drank to fashion new wineskins.[14]

Seerveld goes on to note that whoever is tempted to settle for such an introverted, pietistic Christianity – and it is an easier answer for the older and wiser believers – it is not the Reformed tradition.[15] Which is to say, such a perspective is not found at the root of the scriptural faith emerging from the most consistent stream of the Reformation. Moreover the culture around us *cannot be helped* by such distortion of the biblical mandate. None of this is an appeal to politicize religion (as though salvation were by politics), because a politicized gospel is as great an evil as an ecclesiasticized faith. However, to divorce religion from politics, or from culture in general is a sheer fiction and can no more be done than separating religion from the Church.

What is the Church?

An important question that arises from all this is, what is the Church? And with reference to the question of cultural theology and philosophy, what philosophy is at work in the thinking of those who limit the kingdom of God and direct rule of Christ to the church institute and its activities – who advocate churchianity?

In the scriptures the people of God are identified as those who are called out by the Spirit, gathered together as a body and *appointed to a task*. With the dispersion of the Jews, the synagogue became the centre for worship and instruction for the covenant people – a pattern that was carried over into the Christian era with the local church pattern. In the newer testament the people of God are called the *ekklesia*; a called-out and renewed people likewise appointed to go and bear fruit (John 15:16). Biblically then, the Church is clearly a *people* whose lives in their totality are oriented toward the gospel of the kingdom – this life is evidently much more than the buildings, liturgies and structures of the church institute.

In late-medieval Roman Catholic, or what is often called *scholastic* theology, the church institute and kingdom of

God basically coincide. The church cathedral was called a *basilica* (from the New Testament Greek term for 'royal' or 'king') and was thought to be the realm of Christ, where the church hierarchy was regarded as the means by which Christ exercised his rule and authority. In this line of thinking, one that is still very much with us, no clear distinction is made between the church as *organism* and the church as an *institute*. This results in the ecclesiasticizing of the entire life of the Christian community, clericalism and the spiritual ideal of 'holy orders' and asceticism, which were common phenomena in the medieval world.[16] It was not until the Reformation era that a clear distinction was again made between the church functioning as organism and as institute. Abraham Kuyper crystalizes that distinction:

> The conception of the *instituted church* is much narrower than *the church*...when taken as the *body of Christ*, for [the latter] includes all the powers and workings that arise from re-creation.... The instituted church finds her province bounded by her offices, and these offices are limited to the ministry of the Word, the sacraments, benevolence and church government.... All other expressions of the Christian life do not work by the organs of the special offices, but by the organs of the re-created natural life; the Christian family by the believing father and mother, Christian art by the believing artist, and Christian schools by the believing magister.[17]

In fact, the boundaries and limitations placed by God upon the church *institute* reflect the outward-facing purposes that the Sabbath church *service* serves. Because Christ Jesus in his resurrection life and power is the head of a new race and the founder of re-creation (renewal of creation), the day of rest (resurrection Sunday), opens up the new week so that Sabbath teaching and worship is directed toward the kingdom work of the six days ahead. The word 'liturgy' literally means 'public work.' Public worship prepares us for the very public cultural task ahead. The worshipping community on a Sunday is not directed only toward personal piety and getting the faithful to heaven. Rather it is the place where God's people are prepared for the liturgy of life in all creation (Rom. 12:1). As such the church *institute* is established so that the church as *organism* can live out its kingdom life in the world.

The church institute is *service to this purpose*, it is not to be a power centre existing to serve, expand and enrich itself. Consider that in the older testament the tithe was paid to the *Levites*, who had a varied social and educational function in the cultural life of the Hebrews (cf. Num. 18:21-26), rather than to the *priests*. This biblical scenario reveals that the institutional worship of the people received *a tithe of the tithe*, restricting both the size and power of the priestly office. The church institute is not an end in itself and does not exhaust the scriptural understanding of the kingdom.

The church therefore has two clear modes of existence. The church is manifest in temporal reality as both institute and organism. It is a worshiping community – an *institute* with various offices and ministries – and it is an *organism* – a living *body of believers* engaged daily in the non-ecclesiastical areas of life in service to Christ. We can certainly say that the church is a *unique* body, instituted by Christ, of which he is head. The Lord himself gave it an organizational expression in the apostolic office and sacrament.

This body of Christ is first the *invisible church*. Then it is also the *visible church,* which is the historical manifestation of the invisible body, seen organically in every area of life. Finally, the *institutional church* is the local organisation and expression of that body of believers in a worshipping community with its functioning offices. The visible church thus embraces more than any particular church denomination; it is found wherever God's people are living faithful Christian lives in each area of life. Moreover, and critically for the purposes of this discussion, the body of Christ is manifest across the full range of societal relationships, of which the local church institute is but one.

Although the institutional church is of a special character, the kingdom of God and the visible church are clearly not identical. In fact, Christ and his disciples were found preaching the gospel of the kingdom, and people were entering into it, long before any local churches were established and before there was any institutional expression of it in terms of church government. Nor are the *invisible* church and kingdom of God identical, because the rule and reign of Christ, the ruler of the kings of the earth (Ps. 2; Rev. 1:5), is not limited to those who love and obey him. That rule cannot be restricted to Christian people in their personal relationships, but extends to the entirety of created reality and all that believers do and form within God's world. Kuyper famously said that "there is not a single square inch of the entire universe of which Christ the sovereign Lord of all does not say 'This is mine!'" In view of this and over against Mark Dever's truncated view of discipleship, Gordon Spykman writes, "it is our obligation to honor this claim [i.e. of Christ's total Lordship and sovereignty] and to press it whenever and wherever possible. This calls for political discipleship, academic discipleship – in short, for all sorts of cultural discipleships. This constitutes a truly staggering agenda."[18]

Such an agenda for discipleship seems startling to modern evangelicals nurtured on churchianity. The notion that the Christians confrontation with systematic *unbelief* in culture should be responded to with systematic and comprehensive *belief* is simply foreign. This is in large measure due to a fundamental doubt in the evangelical mind that a specifically Christian view or approach to anything in culture in general is really necessary. After all isn't 'common grace' enough? This idea is usually vague enough to mean that the vast majority of things in life, from education to politics and art, can be dealt with in abstraction from the Christian world-and-life view – that is in a neutral way.

On the one hand, men and women, believers or not, cannot think themselves loose from God's world. By virtue of creation and being made in God's image, human beings are compelled to deal with the real world as God has made it, even in their apostasy, and this does mean we may often find ourselves in broad agreement with non-Christians in a variety of areas. Common Grace, or better Creation Grace, simply means that even after the Fall, the creational structures in which we continue to live and find meaning remain valid in order to maintain creatural existence. Laws which govern motion, growth, thought, sexual distinctions and so forth persisted despite sin. The entrance of sin, however, struck at the direction of lives – sexual acts, thought acts, acts of motion and so forth. So the Christian response to the radical misdirection of the Fall must be a comprehensive Christianity – Christ's saving grace, into every area of life. Just because unbelievers do not all suppress the truth to the same degree and, acting in orderly ways graciously preserved within the creation ordinances, often stumble upon many wonderful secrets of the creation, does not mean we are excused as Christians from systematically manifesting the saving grace of Christ in each area of life. But the conserving gift of Common Grace is all too often made into a complete dis-grace by Christians who refuse to obey the gospel of God by bringing all of life into subjection to the Word of God. Seerveld has said it well:

> [God's conserving work] does not permit the newborn Christian to be satisfied with a common grace culture Christianized. For then the Christian would be denying that the good news has the power to set radically right what sin has misdirected and unbelievers are prostituting, however honorably. The Christian would then be selling the peculiar birthright we share as children of Christ, the right to be the proper lords of creation's development, if the gospel was not allowed to shed its full light

> for time-bound re-creation as well as for eternal salvation…; it
> is a regrettable mistake to think that because our gracious God's
> cosmonomic theatre allows all humanity to act coherently that
> this absolves the Christian community from our special calling
> to praise God ourselves, wholly, unreservedly, in the bonds-
> bursting power of the Holy Spirit.[19]

What Seerveld is rightly resisting here is the synthesizing
motive of churchianity which wants to use robbery from anti-
Christian culture as a synthetic solution to the Christian life
– to regard the church institute as the only distinctly Christian
sphere of life and simply adopt the world's way of doing
politics, medicine, law, art, education and much else besides
in the name of Common Grace with the saving grace of Christ
perhaps sprinkled here and there as a condiment. This is
indeed a dis-grace. But it appears acceptable when we do not
recognise that all "societal relations are required to express
in this temporal life the fullness of our religious principle of
life…, all the spheres in which we function must be permeated
with the Christian life principle."[20] The body of Christ, the
universal and organic covenant people of God, can only reject
this requirement to make all things holy to the Lord if we view
the earth as completely destitute after the Fall and simply a
stage for the church institute to battle through its 'spiritual' life
as pilgrims on the way to somewhere else. But this is surely not
the biblical picture. As Kuyper wrote:

> The world after the fall is no lost planet, only destined now to
> afford the Church a place in which to continue her combats;

and humanity is no aimless mass of people which only serves the purpose of giving birth to the elect. On the contrary, the world now, as well as in the beginning, is the theatre for the mighty works of God, and humanity remains a creation of His hand, which, apart from salvation, completes under this present dispensation, here on earth, a mighty process, and in its historical development is to glorify the name of Almighty God.[21]

If this is the scriptural position regarding God's sovereignty over all men and all of history, and I believe it is, what is the fountainhead of the idea that the church institute and its work is essentially identical with the kingdom of God, reducing the Christian calling to the sole task of 'witnessing,' and providing discipleship for believers' 'personal spiritual life?' What led to the view that planting more churches practically exhausts the mandate of God's people? In short, what is the religious root of churchianity?

The Philosophical Foundations of Churchianity

We saw in passing that according to scholastic theology the church institute coincides completely with the kingdom of God, giving rise to the ecclesiasticizing of life ubiquitous in the medieval Roman Catholic view of reality. However, as we will see, the churchianity that persists amongst many evangelicals in our age posits an even more radical ecclesiasticizing of life, where the link between creation and redemption, which scholastic thought struggled to maintain, has been all but severed. In both cases, lying beneath this dualistic perspective is actually a *non-Christian* philosophy of life. The scholastic tradition essentially sought to christianize the pagan Greek view of nature (composed of form and matter), in order to forge, via this synthesis, a meaningful connection between the 'credible' philosophical views of the ancient world (especially in the thought forms of Aristotle) and the gospel. In fact in 1263, Pope Urban IV reminded Christian scholars that a decree of Pope Gregory IX, which forbade the teaching of Aristotle as mediated by the Arabs, at the same time called on them to interpret Aristotle for the Christian faith:

> William of Moerbeke and Thomas Aquinas were summoned
> to the papal court to assume the task of assimilating Aristotle
> into the Christian world of thought. Aquinas' purpose
> reflected a supreme confidence...shared by many, that an
> establishment of Christian truth upon the foundation of the
> reason of autonomous man was possible.[22]

However, in reality, the Aristotelian concept of nature and of man cannot be reconciled with the biblical view of man as God's image-bearer and the free act of creation – the calling into being of the totality of reality from nothing – by the triune and totally sovereign God.

On the ancient Greek view, nature was the product of impersonal divine reason giving form to an uncreated matter; these two poles stood over against each other. Greek thought saw nature as composed of form – spirit or idea – and matter. In this dualism, matter was the lower realm and spirit, idea or form the higher, superior realm. Consequently, for many Greek thinkers, the body was a prison for the soul from which one ought to seek escape. Early Gnostics, and Marcionite heretics in the early church, expressed this dualism both by denigrating the body and creation – some claiming that the material world was created by a lesser god or demiurge – and by driving a wedge between the older and newer testaments, between law and gospel, creation and redemption. The one belonged to the lower realm of matter, the other to the higher realm of idea and spirit.

When certain Christian philosophers like Thomas Aquinas later tried to harmonize Christianity with Greek thought, on the basis of an unfallen reason, they essentially adopted the Greek view of nature as *form and matter* but added that in order for man to truly understand himself and his spiritual nature, in order to be truly fulfilled and saved, grace must be *added*. With the intellectual soul being absolute form, man's knowledge and understanding of reality in terms of independent reason was fine as far as it went i.e. for all the ordinary stuff of life – for philosophy and education, science and art, politics and government. However, for 'spiritual life' and the way of salvation, that is, for the realm of faith, man needed the addition of grace – a *super*natural addition. In short, on top of nature one needed a *second storey* to complete life. Grace must be added in order to perfect nature. In this way the scholastic tradition sought to *maintain a link* between the gospel of redemption in Christ, and a philosophical view of nature inherited from Greek philosophy.

This attempted synthesis of incompatible views led to the emergence of the idea of a *secular* and *sacred* realm, one ruled over by reason and natural law, the other by grace and special revelation. This gave the church institute the roles of mediator of salvation in the *sacred* realm (the church or kingdom of God) and 'spiritual director' of society when playing the role of chaplain to a *secular* government which went about its common tasks in terms of the dictates of reason. At times nature and grace, or emperor and pope, battled it out for supremacy in terms of who anointed whom.

However, in the fourteenth century, a Franciscan monk named William of Ockham denied there was a real point of contact between the realms of nature and grace. Aquinas had tried to tie the Greek concept of nature to the faith of the church, but Ockham denied that these could be held together. He held to the idea of a divine arbitrariness; human reason could not find out nor prove God. Belief in God was simply a matter of faith, not of knowledge. And so cutting the link between nature and grace, knowledge and faith, between creation and redemption, he rejected the idea of Christianized society, holding to the complete sovereignty of *secular* government. In many respects Ockham anticipates the modern period of history, shunting off the *super*natural Christian life, the realm of faith and revelation, to another world and privatizing Christianity to the church and individual believer. The twentieth-century Dutch Christian philosopher Herman Dooyeweerd observes that Ockham's criticism of the nature-grace link left two options for Christians:

> One could either return to the scriptural ground motive of the Christian religion or in line with the new motive of nature severed from the faith of the church establish a modern view of life concentrated in the religion of the human personality. The first path led to the reformation; the second path led to modern humanism.[23]

Although we rightly associate the Reformation with Martin Luther, the Lutheran and Calvinistic view of the relationship of the gospel with culture, of creation and redemption, and consequently of the mission of God's people, developed in very different directions. Luther himself was educated in Ockham's view of things when at the Erfurt monastery. In fact Luther openly declared, "I am of Ockham's school," and continued Ockham's sharp distinction between *natural* life and *super*natural Christian life. It is no surprise then that we do not find in Luther an intrinsic connection between the Christian faith and one's earthly life.

We see the same dualism expressed in Luther's strong law-gospel opposition – another persistent error in modern evangelicalism. Here the Christian has nothing to do with the law for the law is for the sin 'nature' and is viewed in almost antithetical relationship to grace. The law is stripped by Luther of its function and importance as creational ordinance. As Dooyeweerd has pointed out, "He did not acknowledge a single link between nature, taken with its lawful ordinances, and the grace of the gospel."[24] Accordingly, redemption was seen as the *death* of nature rather than its renewal and rebirth. It is certainly the case that Luther rejected monasticism, but he is radically inconsistent; "Luther even contrasted *God's will as the creator* who places a person amidst the natural ordinances with *God's will as the redeemer* who frees a person from the law."[25]

Following the scholastic thinkers and despite famously calling 'reason' a whore, for Luther, 'reason' remained the guide for the realm of *nature* and there was no point of contact between this 'reason' and the revelation of God's Word. In the vein of Ockham, he regarded secular government, social order and justice as belonging to the domain of reason, not revelation.

Although Luther was not thoroughly consistent and clearly saw a place for God's commandments in society because of the context of Christendom he inhabited, nonetheless, a radical sacred-secular divide remained in Luther's thought, with ecclesiastical life identified with the kingdom of God. What was proper to the distinctly Christian life was the realm of grace, expressed in Word and sacrament in the church, but justice, beauty and the like belonged to the realm of the sinful nature.

Like many Christians before him, Luther did not recognize that the totality of a person's life and thinking *in every area* arises from a religious root. The result was that in Lutheran thought, a divide ran through the centre of reality. Worldly life belonged to the realm of nature and law and as such was troubled by an inner tension with the gospel of love that belonged to a higher *super*natural realm. This tension remains entrenched in the thinking of many modern evangelicals who oppose law to grace or gospel and who regard most of 'secular' life as religiously neutral and governed by principles other than the Word of God. There is no intrinsic point of contact for most evangelicals today between their vocation or cultural life and the Word of God – they belong to almost sealed domains. Moreover, creation itself is consistently viewed as something to be finally escaped; at the very least it is a devalued realm destined to be destroyed and so again a tension runs through the lives of modern evangelicals between the sacred call to holiness given by the church and their life everywhere else. Creation and redemption are essentially cut off from each other.

Many modern theologians, notably Karl Barth, went on to develop a perspective that openly opposed the scriptural idea (cf. Romans 1; Acts 17) that there is no neutrality, that in fact a *religious antithesis* is found in all aspects of life in the world. As a result, Barth and others in his stream of thought rejected the notion of Christian politics, scholarship and education, ecclesiasticizing and privatizing the Christian life. Barth presses the logic of Greek dualism and argues that the Word of God is *wholly other*, with no point of contact between nature/creation and grace. Life in the world is then viewed exclusively in terms of the Fall. As the doctrine of creation recedes from view, knowledge of the ordinances of creation is lost and creation and redemption are separated so as to divide God's will as creator and God's will as redeemer. Consequently, in place of God's law is established a vague and seemingly abstract command to 'love.'

All this is indicative of modern evangelicalism's denial that the totality of God's revelation is relevant to *every area of life* and consequently that there is no such thing as a Christian view of education, law, art, politics, economics, scholarship etc. Most of today's evangelicals have imprisoned the body of Christ, the organic church, and indeed kingdom of God, within the walls of the church institute – its offices and ministries. As a result the gospel itself is redacted to one small element of its full and glorious scope. This intellectual lineage reveals that well-intentioned pastors and leaders who strongly influence contemporary evangelicalism, like Mark Dever, are still in the grip of Greek thought as it has come down to them via scholasticism, Lutheranism, pietism and neo-orthodoxy.

RETREATISM, PIETISM AND CHURCHIANITY

Piety is an important quality of the Christian life. It denotes reverence toward God and sincere devotion. But piet*ism* is the tendency to restrict the meaning of the Christian life to personal devotional disciplines and inward spiritual growth. Pietism, which has so afflicted all stripes of modern evangelicalism, was a movement beginning in German Lutheranism, with theological foundations in medieval thought, that quickly spread to the English-speaking world. The pietists tended to see biblical orthodoxy as dead religion and boasted a more spiritual faith focused on the new birth and various devotional exercises. Emphasis was laid on emotion and feeling because doctrine was considered dry and intellectual. There are significant evangelical church movements today that won't sing hymns for this very same reason – they are allegedly too intellectual and get in the way of emotional engagement with God.

All dualism since Ockham, and especially as expressed in pietism, has had the cultural effect of weakening the church and strengthening the state. With its retreat inward, pietism was completely unable to combat the forces of the Enlightenment, just as Lutheranism was found powerless with the rise of the Third Reich. The Enlightenment perspective saw the state, not the church, as the truly universal institution; the church was the area of *private* faith, whereas the state was the realm of *reason*.

The state would therefore assert itself as the new arbiter of order. Given pietism's primary concern for 'spiritual life,' it did not contest this claim. The same is true of modern evangelical pietism. It has allowed the state to move into and control most of life, and we have given up the majority of that ground uncontested. While on the one hand emphasizing the church and spiritual life, pietism actually allows the church to become an essentially peripheral institution, irrelevant to life in the world.

Pietism also typically derides pleasure in life and the world, viewing this present world as comparatively unimportant. Pietists often refused to enjoy good food, marital sex, beauty and indeed life's many joys, with clear parallels to medieval asceticism. Out of such a distorted view of reality pacifistic ideals also emerged, according to which being killed by thugs assaulting you in the street or being slain by invading military forces is preferable to killing one of the attackers, since the pietist knows he is going to heaven but the hoodlum may not know Christ and would therefore go to hell. This kind of pious sentimentality is commonplace in today's evangelicalism, where God's law is neither known, nor regarded as important. The salvation of individuals from hell is seen as the preeminent concern for the pietist, not the glory, justice and kingdom rule of God. From its inception pietism was implicitly antinomian, seeing no place for God's law-Word. And yet, modern pietistic evangelicalism is divided up into numerous groups, denominations and communions all too ready to condemn one another for not being holy or spiritual enough, too charismatic or too reformed and doctrinal, rather than focusing on bringing every area of life and thought into captivity to Christ.

An immediate offspring of this dualism and pietism is retreatism. Modern churchianity seems to overlook many of the clear demands of Scripture. In Matthew 10:8 we are told, "the kingdom of heaven is at hand. Heal the sick, cleanse the lepers, raise the dead, cast out demons. Freely you have received, freely give." In 1 Corinthians 6 the believers are told to establish courts of arbitration to judge God's people in terms of God's Word. We also see the believers in Acts caring for the poor, widows, and orphans. The early church quickly launched hospitals, care homes for abandoned children, schools, homes for the elderly without families, and much else besides. It was not a church in retreat from the world, but an organic body determined to live out the life of the kingdom, teaching and discipling all the nations in terms of everything Christ commanded. Long before the church was permitted to own buildings for worship, it had established a variety of institutions to meet needs. R. J. Rushdoony has incisively commented:

> The personal impulse, and theologically grounded faith, that we have an obligation under God to minister to human needs, to bring every area of life under Christ's dominion and God's law, and the duty to make God's earth His kingdom, all this has been abandoned as the church has retreated into the position of a mystery religion or cult. All the world is surrendered to evil, and only a little corner, the church and the people in it, represent Christ's domain. How will Christ the king treat a

church that hands His world over to His enemies? ... It is amazing how many people there are who actually believe they are holier and purer because they have surrendered one area after another to Christ's enemies.[26]

Because the church *institute* is rightly limited in its role and jurisdiction in the Christian life and human society, whenever and wherever an unscriptural dualism reigns, where artificial divisions of nature and grace, law and gospel, creation and redemption are propounded, God and his Word become theoretically imprisoned in the church and Christ's reign is faithlessly limited to one sphere of life.

The Recovery of Christianity

If the church institute is identified simplistically with the body of Christ and with the kingdom of God, then clearly the rule of Christ is only possible over that single institute. Moreover the gospel itself becomes wholly church-oriented – saving people for heaven and safety within the worshipping community until Christ returns.

But Christianity, the true gospel of the kingdom, cannot be locked up within a single institution any more than it can be corralled into the enclosure of individual salvation from the consequences of sin. For salvation, which implies total wholeness and restoration, is also *deliverance* from the power and corruption of sin. The scope of salvation is as broad as the scope of the Fall. Clearly then the faith of the gospel is centred in Christ himself, not an institution. This is why we are called *Christians* and our faith *Christianity*, not churchianity. As Willem Ouweneel has pointed out in his criticism of Darryl Hart:

> As long as we do not see the difference between the calling of the church [institute] and the calling of individual Christians, we will not make any progress in these things. For instance

Hart tells us that the Bible "is the guide for church life," and not "for political life." This is a fundamental mistake. The Bible is the guide for Christian life, which is a far wider notion than just church life. Would Hart deny that the Bible is a guide for Christian husbands and Christian wives, and for Christian parents and Christian children? And why not for Christian employers and Christian employees (cf. Eph. 5:25-6:9)? And why not for Christian politicians, or Christian businesspersons? ... The Bible is our starting point for developing a Christian worldview in which we investigate the creation ordinances for marriages, families, schools, companies, and so on...; for non-church life we do not rely only on reason and prudence, as he (following good scholastic traditions) asserts, but on scripture, as well as a Christian worldview rooted in scripture.... The church is not the "special community that renders worship to God." Christians render worship to God at all times, in all circumstances.[27]

In so much of the evangelical community today *churchism* and *churchianity* have replaced Christianity. In Christianity, believers are living out, applying and asserting the Lordship and salvation-victory of Christ for every area of life, rooted in the scriptures.

The gospel is the wisdom and power of God according to the Bible, for Christ is the wisdom, the glory and power of God made manifest. His kingdom and rule is unlimited and extends over all the cosmos – of things visible and invisible, in this age and the one to come (See Col. 1; Eph. 1). Such wisdom in Christ and the gospel cannot be restricted to the church institute any more than the meaning of the reconciliation of all things to God can be limited to the soul of individual believers. God's wisdom is for all people and nations and it is being manifest to all for the good of all. Surely the manifestation of this wisdom and grace must be the deepest desire of every Christian who loves the Lord with all his being. Seerveld asks the pertinent question:

> How can you live openly in this world, God's cosmonomic theatre of wonder, while the (common) graciously preserved unbelievers revel in music and drama, painting, poetry and dance, with a riot of color, a deafening sound raised in praise to themselves and their false gods, how can you live here openly and be silent? Are you satisfied with bedlam for God? Where is our concert of freshly composed, holy stringed music? Our jubilant dance of praise to the Lord? What penetrating drama have our hands made? … Human existence is not absurd: we glory in the image of God! The world is not a curse: it is good creation, struggling under sin toward final deliverance…we as a Christian community must serve up the new wine.[28]

The time has come to be done with the retreatist, pietistic and syncretistic gospel of *churchianity* that has led to the radical decay of our culture, the collapse of the Christian calling and the impotence of a politicized church. A new generation of Christians must, in the power of the Holy Spirit, take up the task afresh of being Christian lords in the development of creation and direction of culture as Christ Jesus intends. For this we need true grace and wisdom not only in our churches but in our marriages and families, schools and civic associations, universities and businesses, political parties and guilds. We need the truth of the Christian gospel to permeate family, church and state and every sphere of life as leaven through a loaf. We must boldly proclaim and apply, in detail, the wisdom of God for all domains of life, regarding not only the way of personal salvation, but for the entirety of our lives for the reconciliation of all things to God. Only in this way will the gospel be unhindered and the wisdom and renewing power of God be effectively released again in our time.

ENDNOTES

1   *Westminster Shorter Catechism*, Q&A 1.

2   I say 'vice-gerent' instead of the more common expression 'vice-regent.' Where regency carries the sense of ruling in the place of another, a gerent is one who rules alongside of, and subordinate to, a sovereign power.

3   David Maraniss, *When Pride Still Mattered: A Life Of Vince Lombardi* (New York: Simon & Schuster, 1999), 274.

4   Calvin Seerveld, *A Christian Critique of Art and Literature* (Toronto: Tuppence Press, 1995), 2-3.

5   Although some would say these issues come under the theological rubric of missiology, contemporary missiology has not given sufficient attention to the specific application of Scripture to contemporary cultural and civilizational challenges.

6   P. Andrew Sandlin, "Introducing Cultural Theology," *Doc Sandlin*, last modified July 12, 2017, https://docsandlin.com/2017/07/12/introducing-cultural-theology/.

7   S.U. Zuidema, *Communication and Confrontation* (Assen/Kampen: Royal VanGorcum & J.H. Kok, 1972), 43.

8   Seerveld, *A Christian Critique*, 15

9   See the lecture *Recovering the Foundations of Social Justice*, at www.ezrainstitute.ca.

10 I deal extensively and critically in *The Mission of God: A Manifesto of Hope for Society* (Toronto: Ezra Press, 2016), with the social justice movement within modern evangelicalism.

11 Jonathan Leeman and Mark Dever interview 'On the Mission of the Church,' https://www.9marks.org/interview/episode-25-on-the-mission-of-the-church/ accessed Nov. 16, 2017.

12 Zuidema, *Communication and Confrontation*, 42.

13 Zuidema, *Communication and Confrontation*, 43-44.

14 Seerveld, *Christian Critique*, 4-5.

15 Seerveld, *Christian Critique*, 5.

16 In spite of this, the medieval church was more interested in broader cultural activities than Dever is now.

17 Abraham Kuyper, *Principles of Sacred Theology*, (New York: Charles Scribner's Sons, 1898), 587-88, 590.

18 Gordon J. Spykman, *Reformational Theology: A New Paradigm for Doing Dogmatics* (Grand Rapids: Eerdmans, 1992) 474.

19 Seerveld, *A Christian Critique*, 18-19

20 H. Evan Runner, *Walking in the Way of the Word: The Collected Writings of H. Evan Runner Vol. 1* (Grand Rapids: Paideia Press, 2016), 105.

21 Abraham Kuyper, *Lectures on Calvinism* (Grand Rapids: Eerdmans, 1978), 162.

22 R. J. Rushdoony, *The One and the Many: Studies in the Philosophy of Order and Ultimacy* (Vallecito, CA: Ross House Books, 2007), 198.

23 Herman Dooyeweerd, *Roots of Western Culture: Pagan, Secular and Christian Options* (Grand Rapids: Paideia Press, 2012), 139.

24 Ibid., 140.

25 Ibid., 141.

26 R. J. Rushdoony, *An Informed Faith: The Position Papers of R. J. Rushdoony* (Vallecito, CA: Ross House Books, 2017), 385

27 Willem J. Ouweneel, *The World Is Christ's: A Critique of Two Kingdoms Theology* (Toronto: Ezra Press, 2017), 260.

28 Seerveld, *Christian Critique*, 21-22.